Molly Best

Written by Sue Mayfield

Illustrated by Sonia Holleyman

Rigby

Molly Best was such a pest.

She liked to joke.

She liked to jest.

Grandpa's room

She dried the dog with
Grandpa's vest

and scared the hamster
from its nest.

She tripped her brother
on the rug

and slipped a slug into his mug.

As Granny took her morning nap,
she dropped a frog into her lap.

She popped a balloon with a pin.

She put Dad's slippers in the trash bin.

She made her mother
fume and frown
by messing up her dressing gown.

Hear them moan from east to west,
"Molly Best, you're such a pest!"